Quick and Fun Learning Activities for Four-Year-Olds

Marla Pender McGhee

Teacher Created Materials, Inc.

Illustrated by Sue Fullam and Jose L. Tapia
Cover Design by Larry Bauer
Images© 1996 PhotoDisc, Inc.

SAg 00-643 Child Care May 2000 $6.95

Made in U.S.A.

ISBN 1-55734-557-6

Order Number TCM 557

Table of Contents

Introduction

Your four-year-old is nearly ready for formal schooling, yet she has a long way to go in terms of school readiness. What can you do to help her be ready for school? You can help her build self-confidence and academic readiness in many ways. As you learn and play together through the activities in this book, you will be helping your child build a strong base which will help her throughout life.

Your four-year-old needs the security of boundaries. She needs the freedom to try out different roles and activities, including structured and unstructured time, active and passive activities, and noisy and quiet time, all within safe boundaries. She also needs to know that different rules may apply in different places and at different times. For example, if everyone were to talk at once in a schoolroom, no one would know what anyone else was saying. So your child may have to wait her turn before speaking at school; but at home, we don't usually have to be formally recognized before being allowed to speak. Stop and put yourself in your child's place and explain how things will work before exposing her to a new setting with new rules. Likewise, take the time to fully explain new activities and games, such as those in this book, to increase her chances of success.

Remember that normal development and milestones that are to be reached at certain times are not set in stone. Some children develop some abilities before others of the same age do. Generally speaking, four-year-olds will be on their way to greater coordination of large and small muscle skills and they will begin to enjoy working with and spending time with others. So, use the activities in this book to build your child's self-esteem (including pride in her newly acquired physical skills) and academic readiness, but don't be afraid to add your own touches to the activities. For example, you may want to introduce an activity for your child and her friend to do together, instead of having every activity be carried out by you and your child alone.

Most of all, relax and have fun with your child as you continue to help her navigate the world!

Author's Note

All of the activities in this book are designed to help build a base of knowledge and experience that will help your child succeed in future learning activities; however, it is important that you and your child see these activities as constructive play, rather than "getting ready for school." For a child, work, play, and learning are all the same, so be sure to emphasize the fun aspect of each activity in order to help foster a love of learning that will last a lifetime.

The activities set forth in this book are based on the premise that four-year-olds need activities which build their creativity, dexterity, problem-solving skills, and confidence. As far as possible, the activities within each section are arranged in order from the least to the most complicated.

When your child is developmentally ready for a certain activity, it will hold his attention long enough for him to perform the activity a few times in a row or for at least five to ten minutes. If a particular activity does not hold your child's attention after a couple of demonstrations, it may be a little too soon or a little too late—developmentally—for your child to benefit from the particular activity. To determine whether your child has passed the optimum stage for a particular activity, move to the next activity listed in that section. If your child shows no interest in either activity, you are probably presenting them too soon, in which case you should wait a month or two before trying again.

In addition to the activities listed in this book, four-year-olds generally enjoy the following activities:
- puzzles with five to ten sturdy pieces
- simple board games (especially those without too many rules and which don't involve reading spaces)
- cutting and pasting (draw simple curved and angular shapes for your child to practice cutting)
- construction sets
- blocks
- realistic looking toys which represent grown-up things, such as a small tool set or stethoscope
- having books read to them (especially tall tales and humorous stories)

Remember, even in this modern age, that some of your child's favorite activities can be those which make use of everyday household items and simple toys.

Stuff Around the House

- Paste
- Glue
- Cotton swabs
- Cotton balls
- Markers
- Crayons
- Non-toxic paint
- Paintbrushes
- Pens
- Pencils
- Construction paper
- Drawing paper
- Tissue paper
- Tracing paper
- Wax paper
- Index cards
- Clothespins
- Rubber bands
- Play dough
- Magnets
- Sand
- Magnifying glass
- Tin foil
- Measuring cups
- Measuring spoons
- Mixing bowls
- Plastic cups
- Paper plates
- Funnel
- Food coloring
- Tape recorder/player
- Cardboard
- Balls
- Puppets
- Dress-up clothes
- Mirror
- Seeds
- Potting soil
- Books

Safety Concerns

Parents are most often concerned about their child's safety. From birth until the toddler stage, we find ourselves locking cupboard doors, tying and discarding plastic bags, and basically never taking our eyes off of our children. Unfortunately, it is sometimes assumed that by age four, a child is more capable of staying out of harm's way. This is not so.

While many four-year-olds have learned not to drink poisons or run into the street after a ball, there is a whole new array of dangers facing them. As they evolve into independent, "do it myself" advocates, four-year-olds can become mesmerized by their attempts and lose sight of safety concerns. The worst area is usually the kitchen! By age four, your child will most likely have grown tired of being the helper and want to do it all herself. She will feel perfectly confident with her abilities to use items like the microwave and stove. Be careful! Though you want to give your child as many chances to be independent and successful, safety must prevail. Many injuries occur in the kitchen.

Be equally as cautious with bath time and swimming. Four-year-olds often try to fill their own tub of water for a bath and can be severely burned. Many have taken "Parent and Me" or toddler swim courses, yet they must *always* be supervised when playing in or around water!

Most importantly, never leave your child alone. Though four-year-olds can appear very responsible and aware of safety issues, they are still children and need supervision and guidance in order to mature and make appropriate decisions. Left alone, a "do it myself" four-year-old can easily be hurt by trying to do something that she just isn't big enough to do.

The activities in this book are designed to expose your child to many fun learning experiences. The key to being safe, however, is to protect your child by always being around to assist and reinforce safety concepts with her. Don't take for granted that she will remember all of the safety rules you have taught her. Together, you can learn and review the important safety skills that will assist your child in leading a healthy, happy life.

Fun with Cooking

Introduction

Four-year-olds want to be helpful and to feel useful and needed, so this is a great age to introduce your child to some household tasks which she will enjoy and which will help out the family. This section includes activities to aid in meal preparation and household beautification, while promoting and building your child's self-esteem. She will not only realize that she can do real things to help out around the kitchen, but she will also receive recognition from others for having done so. Two of the activities in this section, "Sifting Hot Chocolate Mix" and "Kitchen Collage," can also be made and given as gifts.

Teaching your child how to do useful activities which contribute to mealtime preparation also makes your job as a parent less stressful and more fun. Instead of trying to cook dinner while your child is bored or restless in another room, you and your child can work together toward a common goal.

Your child will surely enjoy making, as much as the rest of the family will enjoy sampling, the delicious treats such as "Peanut Butter Balls" and "Surprise Cakes" found in this section. For a unique family treat, your four-year-old can make a special breakfast of her very own, "Cinnamon Raisin Rolls."

Using A Grater

Materials

- Plastic grater
- Carrots
- Cheese or toasted bread
- Plastic bowl
- Non-skid placemat

Activity

Four-year-olds love to help! With attention to a few details, such as using a plastic grater instead of a metal one, and an adult cutting off the parts of the food that will not be used, your four-year-old can truly help in dinner preparation. Grated carrots are great in stir-frying or in salads; grated bread can be used as the bread crumbs in many recipes; and of course, there are endless uses for grated cheese. Grating also helps develop hand-eye coordination and the hand muscles, both of which are prerequisites for more advanced learning activities such as writing.

Have your child wash her hands. Help her get out the materials needed and work at a child-sized table. Demonstrate the correct use of a grater. In demonstrating, use the same materials you wish your child to use. Note that it is easier for a child to set a grater in a bowl that has been placed on a plastic non-skid placemat instead of on a plate or piece of wax paper as an adult might use. Have your child demonstrate her understanding of how to grate before you turn half of your attention back to the rest of dinner preparation.

Be sure to talk with your child about what part this grated food will play in the forthcoming meal. Help her to see that she is truly helping with the meal preparation, as opposed to pretending to cook in a toy kitchen while Mommy or Daddy cooks in the real kitchen.

Sifting Hot Chocolate Mix

Materials

- Measuring cups
- Measuring spoons
- Sifter
- Ingredients for mix (See recipe below.)
- Large wooden spoon
- Large plastic bowl
- Storage container
- Funnel (Optional)

Activity

Not only are measuring and sifting useful in and of themselves, they also provide practice in hand-eye coordination and develop the hand muscles. In this case, they even result in a tasty and useful end-product, as the two of you drink yummy hot chocolate!

Help your child prepare the recipe which follows. After demonstrating with one or two of the ingredients, allow him to fill the appropriate measuring cups and spoons with the ingredients. When this mix is all made up, help him put it in the storage container, so you can enjoy the drink at a later time, too.

Ingredients for Hot Chocolate Drink Mix

1 cup sugar (240 mL)
$1/3$ cup cocoa (160 mL)
1 cup powdered milk (240 mL)
$1/2$ cup powdered coffee creamer (120 mL)
$1/4$ teaspoon salt (1.25 mL)

Directions

Place the sifter in the bowl. Measure the sugar and dump half of it into the sifter. Measure the cocoa and dump half of it into the sifter. Sift it into the bowl. Dump the rest of the sugar and cocoa into the sifter and sift it into the bowl. Measure the powdered milk and dump it into the sifter. Measure the salt and dump it into the sifter. Measure the coffee creamer and dump it into the sifter. Sift into the bowl. Remove the sifter and stir all the ingredients together. Once the ingredients are well mixed, use a measuring cup to scoop up the mix and put it into the storage container. Place two heaping tablespoons of mix in a mug, add hot water, stir, and enjoy!

Bugs on Logs

Materials

- Celery sticks
- Peanut butter or cream cheese
- Raisins
- Plastic knife
- Small towel or dish cloth
- Cutting board
- Non-skid placemat

Activity

"Bugs on Logs" makes a great, nutritious snack or addition to a meal.

To begin, cut off the tops and bottoms of the celery so that long sticks of celery remain. Help your child wash and dry the celery. Move the rest of the materials to a child-sized work space. Demonstrate how to cut the celery into smaller sticks using the plastic knife. Help your child place the cutting board on the non-skid placemat and cut sticks about three to four inches (8-10 cm.) long. Next, help your child spread the peanut butter or cream cheese on the celery sticks. Then, help him place raisins at intervals on top of the spread. Help him clean up and arrange the "Bugs on Log" on a serving platter.

Edible Aquariums

Materials

- Blue gelatin mix
- Measuring cup
- Spoon
- Bowl
- Water
- Gummy fish or sharks
- Clear plastic cups

Activity

This fun snack is great to serve at parties. Imagine your child's sense of pride as her friends exclaim over these treats that she made!

Help your child make gelatin according to package directions—you can do the hot water part, then let your child stir in the cold water. Divide the gelatin evenly and pour it into four clear, plastic cups. Refrigerate them until they are almost set. Then, show your child how to stir in five or six gummy fish or sharks and refrigerate the cups again until serving time.

Note: This recipe makes four servings per package of gelatin.

Setting the Table

Materials

- Placemats
- Utensils
- Napkins

Activity

This is another activity in which your child can truly contribute to mealtime preparation. Before beginning, make or purchase placemats with simple outlines showing where the utensils and napkin should be placed.

Then, show your child how specific outlines represent specific utensils and how to place the correct utensils on the placemat in the correct places. Show him where to place the napkin, as well. Take the other placemats, sets of utensils and napkins, one at a time, and help your child place them properly.

Be sure to let your child know what a help it is for him to contribute to the family's mealtime preparation by doing such a grown-up job. After a month or so of setting the table using these special placemats as guidelines, help your child practice setting the table using regular placemats, without the outlines.

Kitchen Collage

Materials

- Uncooked macaroni
- Uncooked dried beans
- Glue
- Cardboard
- Dark colored marker or crayon

Activity

This collage shows a different way to use some foods in making an attractive decoration. Try to provide your child with two or three varieties of beans and one or two varieties of macaroni.

Demonstrate on the opposite side of the cardboard (an 8 x 8-inch / 20 x 20 cm., piece works well) how to draw a few lines which will separate the surface of the cardboard into different sections. Turn the cardboard over and help your child do as you just demonstrated. Then help her fill in one section with glue. Show her how to choose one kind of bean or macaroni and cover all the glue in that section with the same type of bean or macaroni. Help and encourage her to complete the collage by filling each section, one at a time with glue, then covering the glue with a certain type of bean or macaroni.

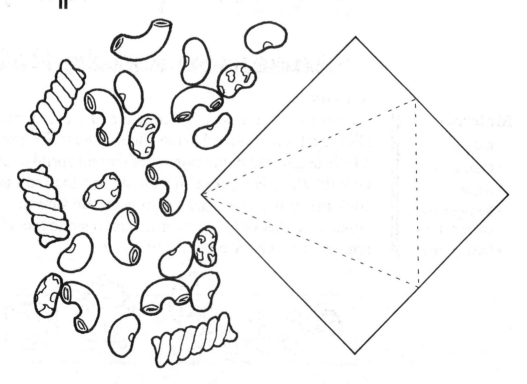

Fruit Kabobs

Materials

- Bananas
- Strawberries
- Grapes
- Toothpicks
- Dull knife
- Cutting board
- Placemat or wax paper

Activity

Working over a placemat or piece of wax paper, help your child assemble the necessary materials. Wash the strawberries and grapes. Slice the banana into chunks and show your four-year-old how to slide the chunks onto a toothpick. The easiest way to do this is to put the fruit on a placemat and stick the toothpick into it. Continue helping your child put one grape, strawberry, and banana chunk onto each toothpick. These fruit kabobs can be used as nutritious snacks for the whole family!

Cinnamon Raisin Rolls

Materials

- Raisins
- Cinnamon
- Sugar
- Refrigerated crescent rolls
- Baking sheet

Activity

Help your child open the package of crescent rolls and place each one onto a baking sheet. Show her how to mix a little sugar and cinnamon together and sprinkle each roll with it. Have her put raisins on top and then roll up and cook the rolls as the package directs. Be sure to emphasize that only a grown-up can operate the oven and remove the treats when they are done.

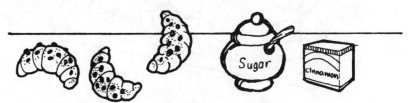

Peanut Butter Balls

Materials

• Ingredients
 (See below.)

Activity

   Help your child mix the ingredients from the recipe below in a plastic, medium-sized bowl. Help him form the mixture into little balls. They can be stored at room temperature for a few days or in the refrigerator for a few weeks. When finished, they make tasty, and nutritious snacks that the whole family will enjoy.

Recipe for Peanut Butter Balls

(Makes 5 dozen)
1 cup (240 mL) peanut butter
1 (240 mL) cup honey
2 cups (480 mL) non-fat dry milk powder
2 cups (480 mL) oatmeal

Crispy Easter Eggs

Materials

- Crispy rice cereal
- Colored marshmallows
- Butter
- Saucepan
- Cotton balls
- Cooling oil
- Baking sheet
- Wax paper
- Plastic Easter eggs

Activity

Follow the directions on the cereal box for making crispy rice cereal treats, but use colored marshmallows instead of white ones. Allow your child to put the first ingredients in the cold saucepan, then do the next part yourself, reminding her that only grown-ups use hot pans and the stove. While you cook, she can use an oil-soaked cotton ball to coat the insides of plastic Easter egg halves.

When the cooked mixture is done, drop it by large spoonfuls onto a baking sheet that is covered with wax paper. Allow it to cool until it is safe for your child to handle. Then help her fill each egg half with the mixture and snap two together to make a filled egg. Put them in the refrigerator for a few hours, then unmold the eggs, taking the shells off, and place the crispy treats on a serving plate. Store them at room temperature. Though this is sticky, your four-year-old is sure to love the egg-shaped, colorful crispy treats.

Surprise Cakes

Materials

- Plain cupcakes
- Icing
- Butter knife
- Gummy candy (Optional)

Activity

Using cooled cupcakes, help your child cut each one in half horizontally. Show him how to put a glob of icing on top of the bottom half and spread it a little. If you'd like, he can hide gummy candies inside the icing for an even greater surprise to the eater. Next, put the top half back onto the bottom, iced-half, so it is like a sandwich. Finally, cover the entire cupcake with icing. This messy project is a great way to let your child help you get ready for a birthday party!

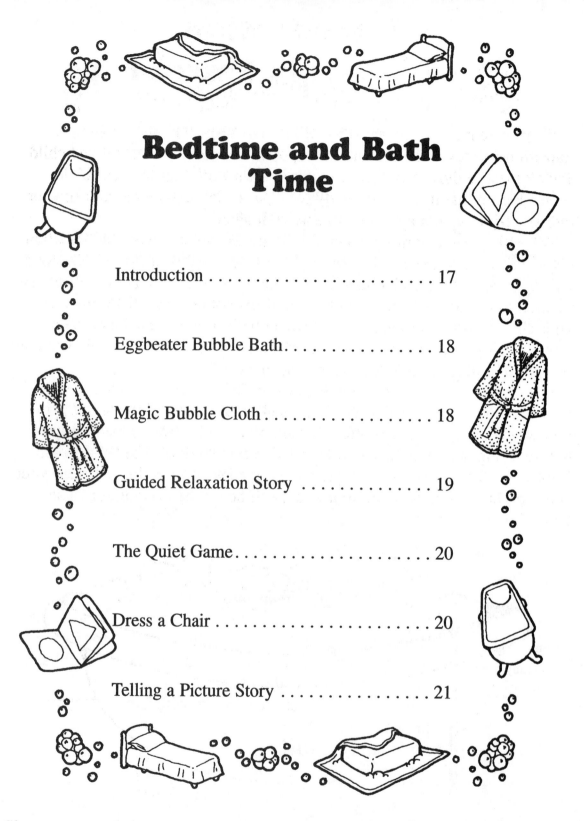

Bedtime and Bath Time

Introduction

Every parent needs to have a lot of ideas to help make these two transitional times smoother and more positive for both the parent and child. Try all these activities and use whichever ones work best for your child, remembering that if he is not ready for a particular activity the first time or two you try it, wait a month or so and try it again.

The bath time activities presented here are designed to ease the transition between an active day and a quiet night. Of course, water is always a good way to calm a child, and a bath (or wading pool in appropriate weather) can be used to soothe an irritable child even if it's not his usual bath time. If your child is going through a phase where he is afraid of the bathtub or doesn't enjoy bath time for some other reason, these enjoyable activities may be used to entice him to enjoy bath time again.

The bedtime activities presented here are designed to facilitate the rest of the transition from an active day to a good night's sleep. Depending upon how keyed up your child is after his bath, you might want to read a story before trying the bedtime activities listed in this section. The "Guided Relaxation Story" activity is appropriate for all four-year-olds, whereas your child might need to be about four and a half before he is ready for "The Quiet Game" activity.

Eggbeater Bubble Bath

Materials

- Eggbeater
- Large plastic bowl
- Non-skid placemat
- Mild liquid soap

Activity

While this activity does use kitchen materials, it is listed as a bath time activity because the bubbles will end up in the bathtub. What better place to make a mess than in the bathtub!

Set a bowl on a non-skid placemat and fill it $1/3$ full of cold water. Add a few tablespoons of liquid soap and place the eggbeater in the bowl, resting it on the bottom. Demonstrate how to use the eggbeater. Hold the bowl for your child while she uses the eggbeater to make a bowl full of bubbles. Remove the eggbeater from the bowl and take it into the bathroom. After you run the bath water, help your child dump the bowl into it. She will be excited about getting in this special bubble bath.

Magic Bubble Cloth

Materials

- Washcloth
- Bar of soap

Activity

Four-year-olds love magical things, so this bit of magic may be good motivation to get your child into the tub.

Wet a washcloth, then squeeze it out a little bit. Rub some soap lightly on a small area in the center of one side of the washcloth. Take and hold a breath, then put the washcloth up to your pursed lips (be sure that the side touching your lips is not the soapy side) and blow. Remove the cloth from your lips to get another breath. Then put it back to your lips as before and blow again. Look at the soapy side of the washcloth. You will have made bubbles appear magically. Encourage your child to bathe with these magic bubbles and let her continue blowing bubbles like you have shown her.

Guided Relaxation Story

Materials

• None

Activity

This activity revives the old-fashioned art of storytelling with a new twist, that of guided relaxation.

Tuck your child into bed and sit near her in her darkened room while you tell a "Guided Relaxation Story."

This type of story is a story you make up as you go along. It should have a peaceful place that your child enjoys as the setting, like the beach or Grandma's backyard.

Tell the story using your child as the main character. Be sure to use your child's full name in the beginning so that she will recognize herself. Allow her a small, but not overly dramatic, adventure within the story. As the story winds down, include your child feeling very sleepy. End the story with your child—as the character in the story—having or getting ready to have good dreams.

The Quiet Game

Materials

- Sand timer (Optional)

Activity

This activity can be done as a prelude to bedtime, helping calm your child, or once your child is in her bed being read to and tucked in.

Tell your child that it is time to play "The Quiet Game." Explain how the game works: "We close our eyes or watch the sand timer for one minute." (Time can vary slightly and can grow longer as your child matures and gets used to this game.) "At the end of that minute/time, we open our eyes and in a quiet voice, we tell each other what we heard."

Note: If your child is going through a stage where she thinks sounds are coming from ghosts or other "bad guys," explain what the noise really was. For example, if the central heat coming on sounds like a ghost to your child, say "I heard that sound too, but don't worry, it was just the heater coming on."

Dress a Chair

Materials

- Clothes for the next day
- Small chair

Activity

What better way to end a day than by preparing for the next. Help your child develop responsibility skills while you ease the hectic morning schedule of getting her dressed and ready.

Let your child assist you in choosing what she will wear the next day. Consider everything—underwear, shoes, socks, hair accessories, etc. Using a small chair in her bedroom, lay the clothes on the chair, as if dressing it. You'll be surprised at how smooth the morning goes and how your four-year-old takes great pleasure in planning ahead!

Telling a Picture Story

Materials

• Picture book

Activity

Either before or after you read a bedtime story to your child, tell him that you would like for him to tell you a story from a picture book. Encourage him to turn the pages after telling a little about each. You will probably notice that, at first, the sentences about one page will not relate to the next page. But as time goes on, and with your good modeling by reading him stories, your child will begin to tell cohesive stories. He may also tire of his story reading and quit before finishing the pictures. All of this is fine and normal. Allow him to do what he is ready for and, of course, always be sure to thank him for reading/telling you such a good story. You will be amazed at his sense of pride for doing something that you do so regularly for him!

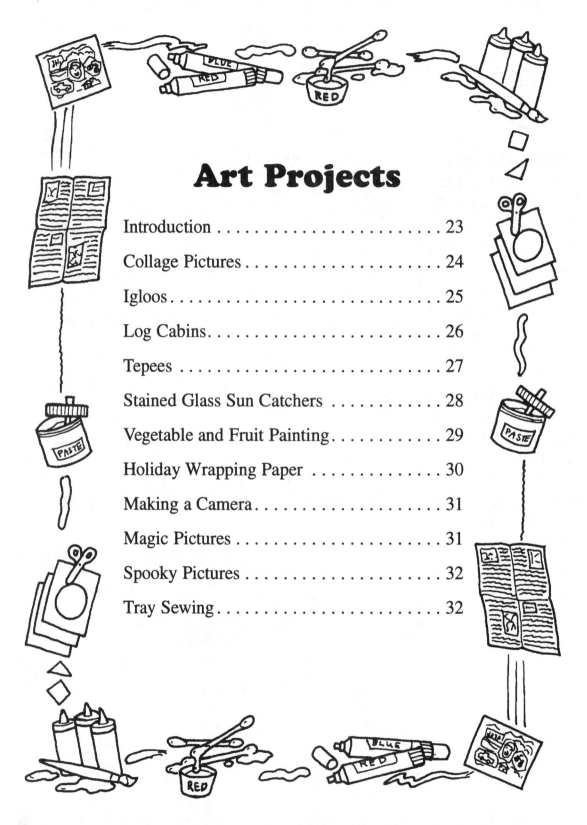

Art Projects

Introduction

Four-year-olds are proud of their abilities, and art projects are great ways to give them a chance for their creations to be admired and praised by others. When working with your child on art projects, be sure to keep the focus on the joy of the process instead of the end-product. It is far more beneficial to explore and enjoy the time together rather than trying to make something perfect. With this in mind, you will see why it is best to guide your child in making his own creation instead of making a sample for him to copy. While not yet as coordinated as you are, your four-year-old is becoming more and more able to use his hands and mind to be creative.

The activities listed in this section entail the use of small hand and finger muscles which will help lead him to greater success in future endeavors such as writing, drawing, and in solving mathematical problems. These art projects are also intended to stimulate your child's creativity and ability to think abstractly, which will both help your child in future problem-solving situations.

The activities in this section will expand your child's world as he uses his imagination. For example, this section includes three multicultural activities which together make up a global village, "Igloos," "Log Cabins," and "Tepees." Activities such as "Magic Picture" and "Spooky Pictures" will expand your four-year-old's understanding of these descriptive words.

Collage Pictures

Materials

- Collage bag
- Heavy paper
- Paste
- Cotton swabs
- Wax paper

Activity

Before beginning, take out or create your own collage bag. A collage bag is a bag you keep on hand and fill with little bits of this and that (scraps of material, pieces of tin foil, scraps of wrapping paper, ribbon, etc.). Over time, your child will have a great resource to use for art projects and will also be participating in recycling.

When the bag is ready, put some paste on a piece of wax paper for your child. To make an abstract collage, show your child how to select one item from the collage bag. Then demonstrate the following pasting technique. Dip one end of a cotton swab into the paste. Pick up the selected piece from the collage bag, rub the pasty end of the swab on the collage piece, and set the collage piece, pasted-side down, onto the heavy paper. Have your child randomly fill up most of the paper using this pasting technique. For an older child, have her draw a simple outline drawing first, using a crayon of the same color as the object to be glued onto the collage. Then help her fill in the drawing by gluing the object down.

In addition to being a fun way to make a beautiful picture, this activity can be great in building the self-esteem of a child who is frustrated when her drawings don't look the way she intended.

Igloos

Materials

- Yogurt container
- Marsh-mallows
- Icing
- Cardboard
- Glue

Activity

Build your child's cultural awareness by talking to him about how houses are built in places where it snows a lot and stays very cold. Explain that igloos are really made out of big blocks of snow that look like big marshmallows. Also explain that igloos are much bigger than what you're making today, that they are big enough for people to live inside them. You can explain that you are making your igloo out of marshmallows and icing because snow would melt inside your nice warm house. A wonderful story to extend this activity is *Mama, Do You Love Me?* by Barbara M. Josse. Check with your local library to see if they have it.

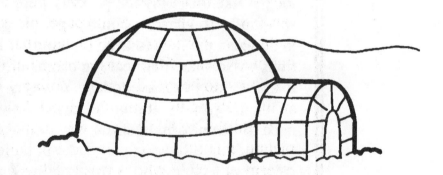

Cover a yogurt container with a thin coating of icing, then cover icing with marshmallows. Be sure to put a little icing on the sides of the marshmallows too, so that they will stick to each other as well as to the yogurt container.

This and the two activities which follow can be used to create a global village, thereby expanding your child's cultural awareness.

Log Cabins

Materials

- Large pretzel rods
- Icing
- Cardboard
- Construction paper

Activity

Place two pretzel rods parallel to each other on a piece of cardboard, "gluing" them down lengthwise with icing. Then place two more pretzel rods opposite these but on top, so the ends of the new ones are on top of the ends of the first two, thereby creating a square. Then "glue" these by putting icing on top of where the ends overlap. Keep building in this manner until all the pretzel rods are used. (The walls will be six pretzels high.) Fold a piece of construction paper in half lengthwise. Then open it back up and set it on top of the log cabin to function as the roof.

You can build your child's historical awareness by explaining to him that people used to live in houses that looked like this, only the pretzels were logs and the icing was mud. You can explain that people packed extra mud in between the logs to keep out cold air in the winter time. Also share that real log cabins are much bigger than the one you made today. You may want to make another log cabin later out of twigs, however, the twigs need to be uniform in size.

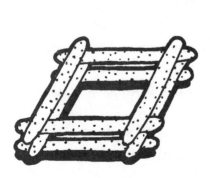

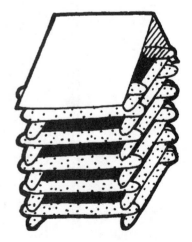

Tepees

Materials

- Round oatmeal box
- Pretzel rods
- Icing
- Fruit roll-ups
- Cardboard

Activity

Build your child's cultural awareness by explaining to her that some of the first people to live in America lived in houses called tepees that looked like what you will be building. Explain that the pretzels were really logs, the fruit roll-ups were animal hides, and the tepees were bigger than what you're making today. They were big enough for people to live in them.

Cut an empty oatmeal box in half so that you have two cylinders. Glue one cylinder upright on a piece of 8 x 8 inch (20 x 20 cm.) cardboard. Use icing to secure pretzel rods intermittently around one oatmeal box cylinder. Put a little icing (about $\frac{1}{2}$ teaspoon / or 2.5 mL) on the bottom of each pretzel rod and secure each near the top of the cylinder with $\frac{1}{2}$ to 1 teaspoon (2.5 to 5 mL) of icing. Be sure that the pretzel rods lean in at an angle, so all the top ends are close together. Next, unroll one fruit roll-up for the teepee and use it to cover the outside, overlapping it slightly and securing it with a thin coating of icing spread along the pretzel rods.

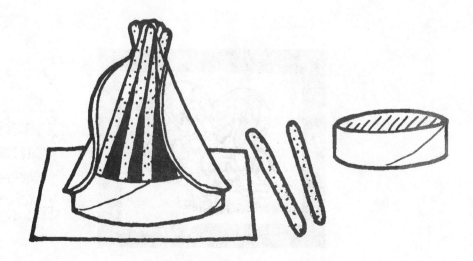

Stained Glass Sun Catchers

Materials

- Tracing paper
- Construction paper
- Light colored non-toxic markers
- Cotton balls
- Baby oil
- Glue stick

Activity

Have your child draw a picture on a piece of tracing paper. Be sure she fills up the whole page. While she is doing this, cut a "frame" for the sun catcher by folding a piece of construction paper that is the same size as the tracing paper in half and cutting out the inside, leaving about one inch (2.5 cm.) all the way around. Unfold the construction paper and set it aside. When your child has finished using the markers to make her picture, help her put a little baby oil on a cotton ball and rub it on the back of the tracing paper. (Using unexpected materials in an activity such as baby oil, helps expand your child's creative thinking as it shows a new use for a particular material.) Next, help her rub the glue stick on one side of the frame that you cut, then help her place the picture inside it, folding it again to complete a frame. Allow the glue to dry, then tape the framed picture to a sunny window. This beautiful sun catcher will truly resemble stained glass as the sun streams through it.

Vegetable and Fruit Painting

Materials

- Three or four fruits or vegetables
- Washable, thick paint
- Construction paper
- Newspaper

Activity

There are as many variations of this activity as there are combinations of various colors, fruits, and vegetables. Just be sure not to use a fruit or vegetable that is too juicy. Also be sure your child wears a paint apron or old clothes while doing this activity, and choose construction paper that is a different color than the paint. Using vegetables and fruits with different shapes and textures will contribute a lot to this activity. For example, you might want to use a chunk of potato, a chunk of carrot, or an apple cut in half widthwise. Star fruit also makes a nice print. You can also cut some of the fruit away to make a shape print, as the picture below shows.

Before beginning, set a piece of construction paper down for your child to use as the base for his picture. Lay sheets of newspaper under the construction paper to catch extra paint. Show him how to hold a chunk of fruit or vegetable in one hand and dip one end or side of it into the paint. Help him press it, with the paint-side down, onto the construction paper. Do the same with all the different fruits and vegetables you have prepared.

Holiday Wrapping Paper

Materials

- Newsprint
- One star fruit (carambola)
- Thick, non-toxic green and red paint

Activity

This inexpensive wrapping paper will make gifts all the more valuable for the recipient, as they were handmade by a very special person, your child.

Simply follow the directions for the "Vegetable and Fruit Painting" activity on page 29. However, use large pieces of newsprint to make the prints on, since they are bigger and easier to wrap gifts. Also, only use half of the star fruit in each color, one for red and one for green. Allow the sheets to dry, then use them to wrap holiday gifts.

As an alternative, you can use this procedure with other appropriate fruits/vegetables and appropriate colors to make wrapping paper for many different occasions. Potatoes cut in heart shapes make lovely Valentine's Day and Mother's Day paper when stamped in red or pink paint.

Making A Camera

Materials

- Empty JELL-O® box
- Hole punch
- Glue
- Tape
- Red construction paper
- Black crayon or paint

Activity

Have your child color or paint an empty JELL-O® box black. Then tape the ends shut. Punch a hole in both sides of the box so that your child can hold one hole up to her eye and see all the way through. Have her cut a small circle out of red construction paper and glue it on the right side of the top of the camera. Show her how to hold the camera to her eye, find what she wants to take a picture of, and push the red button, saying "Click." Smile!

Magic Pictures

Materials

- Cotton swabs
- Lemon juice
- White paper
- Light bulb

Activity

Tell your child that he can make magic pictures that will be invisible at first but that you will help him see them later. Simply have him use lemon juice on cotton swabs to paint a picture on white paper. When he is done, emphasize that only you, a grown-up, can do the part to make the picture show. As the adult, hold the paper a few inches above a shining light bulb. Your child will be amazed as he sees his magic picture! He may also like the idea of sending a mystery magic picture, along with instructions for decoding it, to a relative or friend.

Spooky Pictures

Materials

- White paper
- Crayons
- Paintbrush
- Black paint

Activity

Have your child draw a crayon picture that covers the entire white paper she is working on. If she wants white spaces, have her color them white. Tell her that for this special "Spooky Picture," she needs to color very hard and cover the whole paper with crayons. When she is done, have her paint lightly over the picture with thin, watered-down black paint. The picture will now be spooky. Oooooh!

This same activity can be done as a rainy day picture, using watered-down blue paint, or as a sunny day picture, using yellow paint.

Tray Sewing

Materials

- Styrofoam tray
- Yarn
- Embroidery needle

Activity

Before starting the activity with your child, file down the end of an embroidery needle and thread it with yarn. Using a clean, Styrofoam tray, like those found with produce or meat, show your child how to make a sewing picture by sewing with the yarn on the Styrofoam tray. In the beginning, her pictures will just be free-form designs, but as she becomes more adept at this technique, she may prefer to draw the picture first on the tray and then sew on the lines.

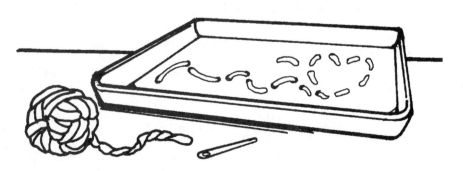

Music and Movement

Introduction

Music and movement activities such as those listed in this section allow your child to make use of her need to move around at this age. As she moves purposefully, rather than randomly, she is training her body to respond to the will of her mind. This will become increasingly important as she is placed in more formal situations requiring certain behaviors.

As your four-year-old is exposed to music, she begins to incorporate the pleasure and science of music into her everyday world. This is a good age for a child to begin some type of music lessons as well, before she begins to think of the ability to make music as something mysterious that only a few people are able to do. Everyone can create and enjoy music to some degree if exposed to it early enough. Encourage your child to learn and express her musical interests. Who knows? You may have the next Beethoven on your hands.

Among the many benefits of the Music and Movement activities, here are two more! Body poems such as "I Have A Nose" and "On My Head" help increase your child's awareness of her body and body image. Songs such as "The Hammer" and "AEIOU" help prepare your child for later number and letter activities. Enjoy!

The Hammer Song

Materials

- "The Hammer Song" (See below.)

Activity

Performing these types of poems helps develop the memory and sense of sequence, as well as some number concepts and anatomical references. Research has shown that when words are performed along with actions, memorization is quicker and longer lasting.

Begin by sitting on the floor, with your back straight, knees bent, feet on the floor in front of you, and fists resting on either side of you. Have your child sit next to you, just as you are, and teach her the following words (using her name instead of Jenny) and actions to the tune of "Johnny Works with One Hammer."

The Hammer

Actions should be done continuously during each verse.

Verse 1: Jenny works with one hammer, one hammer, one hammer. Jenny works with one hammer. Then she works with two.
Action: Bring one fist up and down beside you, bending at the elbow.

Verse 2: Jenny works with two hammers, two hammers, two hammers. Jenny works with two hammers. Then she works with three.
Action: Bring both fists up and down, on either side of you.

Verse 3: Jenny works with three hammers, three hammers, three hammers. Jenny works with three hammers. Then she works with four.
Action: Bring both fists up and down on either side of you and bring one foot up and down in front of you.

Verse 4: Jenny works with four hammers, four hammers, fours hammers. Jenny works with four hammers. Then she works with five.
Action: Bring both fists and both feet up and down.

Verse 5: Jenny works with five hammers, five hammers, five hammers. Jenny works with five hammers. Then she goes to sleep!
Action: Bring both fists and both feet up and down and nod your head up and down. Roll over on your side and pretend to go to sleep.

I Have a Nose

Materials

- "I Have a Nose" poem (See below.)

Activity

Teach your child the words and actions to this poem by standing up and performing it with him. Use encouragement as you continue to help him learn it.

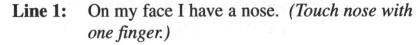

I Have a Nose

Line 1: On my face I have a nose. *(Touch nose with one finger.)*

Line 2: And way down here I have 10 toes. *(Bend over and touch toes with both hands.)*

Line 3: I have two eyes that I can blink. *(Point to both eyes with both fingers.)*

Line 4: I have a head to help me think. *(Touch head with one finger.)*

Line 5: I have a chin and very near *(Touch chin with one finger.)*

Line 6: I have two ears to help me hear. *(Touch both ears with both fingers.)*

Line 7: I have a mouth with which to speak. *(Point to mouth with one finger)*

Line 8: And when I run I use my feet. *(Tap feet.)*

Line 9: Here are arms to hold up high. *(Hold up both arms.)*

Line 10: And here's a hand to wave good-bye. *(Wave with one hand.)*

I Can Jump

Materials

- "I Can Jump" poem (See below.)

Activity

Learning to follow directions and control one's self is vital when starting school. Make the transition easier for your child by doing this simple activity. It is not only fun but will help your child learn to follow directions while building his self-esteem with reminders of all the things he can do.

Begin in a standing position and have your child do the actions that you say to him.

I Can Jump

Line 1: I can jump, jump, jump.

Line 2: I can hop, hop, hop.

Line 3: I can clap, clap, clap.

Line 4: I can stop, stop, stop.

Line 5: I can nod my head for "yes."

Line 6: I can shake my head for "no."

Line 7: I can bend my knees a little bit.

Line 8: And sit. . . down. . . slow!

After your child gets used to following your commands, give him a chance to be the leader and direct you. Have fun!

On My Head

Materials

- "On My Head" poem (See below.)

Activity

This is another poem that will bring a smile to your child's face as she delights in all of the things she can do. It can be done standing or sitting, even in the car! Simply use both hands to do the action described as you recite each line.

Line 1: On my head, my hands I place.

Line 2: On my shoulders, my hands I place.

Line 3: On my face, my hands I place.

Line 4: On my hips, my hands I place.

Line 5: And at my side, my hands I place.

Line 6: Then behind me they will hide.

Line 7: I will hold them up so high.

Line 8: Quickly make my fingers fly.

Line 9: Hold them out in front of me.

Line 10: Swiftly clap—one, two, three.

A-E-I-O-U

Materials

• Words to
A-E-I-O-U
(See below.)

Activity

Your child is sure to love this version of the famous song "B-I-N-G-O." Encourage her to sing along and expose her to some early reading skills.

A-E-I-O-U

There was a school that had some letters and vowels were their names, oh!
A E I O U—A E I O U—A E I O U
And vowels were their names, oh!

There was a school that had some letters and vowels were their names, oh!
clap E I O U—clap E I O U—*clap* E I O U
And vowels were their names, oh!

There was a school that had some letters and vowels were their names, oh!
clap clap I O U—*clap clap* I O U—*clap clap* I O U
And vowels were their names, oh!

There was a school that had some letters and vowels were their names, oh!
clap clap clap O U—*clap clap clap* O U—*clap clap clap* O U
And vowels were their names, oh!

There was a school that had some letters and vowels were their names, oh!
clap clap clap clap U—*clap clap clap clap* U—*clap clap clap clap* U
And vowels were their names, oh!

There was a school that had some letters and vowels were their names, oh!
clap clap clap clap clap
clap clap clap clap clap
clap clap clap clap clap
And sometimes Y and W!

My String Instrument

Materials

- Small box
- Rubber bands
- Plastic tab
  (used to close
  bread bags)

Activity

Help your child remove the lid from the box, then help her stretch and fit the rubber bands over the box so that they form "strings" over the open space in the top. (Using four or five rubber bands of different lengths and thicknesses will help vary the sounds your child can make with his instrument.)

There are three different ways to play this instrument. First, show your child how to "pluck" the strings using the thumb and forefinger. Second, demonstrate how to "strum" the strings by turning your hand over, with fingers together, and running your fingernails backwards across the strands. Encourage your child to try it. Last, demonstrate how to "pick" the strings by holding the plastic tab between the thumb and forefinger with the smooth side down and running it along the strings. Encourage her to try this, too. Then let your child make music of her own, exploring all of the ways to play her string instrument. Be sure to praise her and enjoy the tunes!

Marching with Music Sticks

Materials

- Marching music
- CD or cassette player
- Wooden spoons

Activity

Encourage your child to march with you to the music. Once he has mastered this, introduce the music sticks, or wooden spoons. Demonstrate how to march along while holding the sticks in front of you, as your arms (which are going up and down at opposite times) meet. Hit the sticks together in time to the music and enjoy your mini marching parade!

Hop, Skip, and Jump!

Activity

Materials

• Stop watch

In a clear, safe area, mark a start and a finish line. (Six yards, or five meters, apart will be a good distance.) If your child can hop, skip, and jump, proceed with the following. If he cannot, don't be alarmed! These are gross motor skills that are still developing. You can work on them, but supplement this activity with things he can do, like walking backwards.

Time your child first as he hops on one foot at a time from the start to finish line. Then time his skipping, keeping in mind that skipping is often difficult for four-year-olds. Finally, time his jumping from one foot to both, or both to both. Tell him which way he was the fastest and see if he can beat his scores on a second round. Remember, the emphasis is on having fun, practicing these important movement skills, and trying to beat HIS score. If playing with a friend, do the activity for fun, without timing the races, as competition is not the focus.

_____ Start

_____ Finish

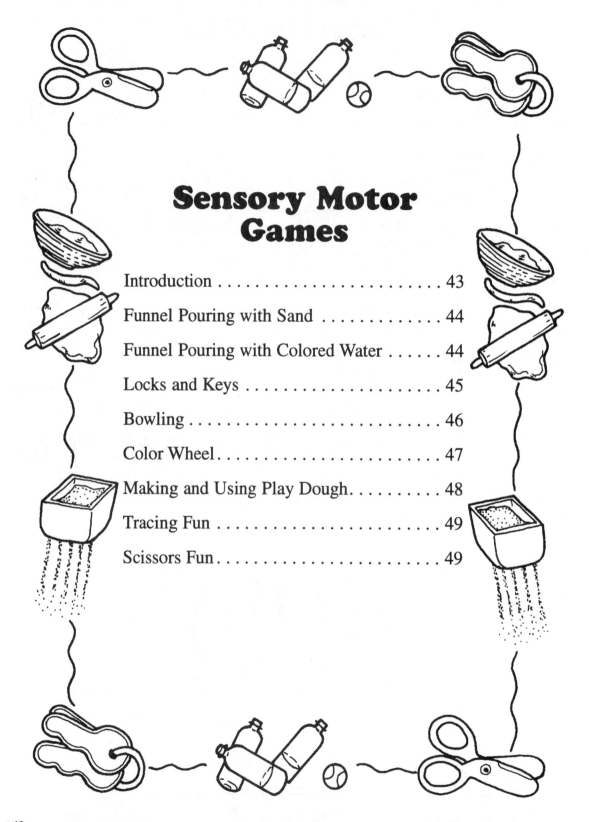

Sensory Motor Games

Introduction

The activities in this section focus on the development of the senses in conjunction with the development of motor skills. Children this age receive much joy through discovery and refinement of their own abilities. They are especially proud when they are able to perfect their physical abilities by doing better and better at physically challenging tasks. For example, many of the activities in this section help your child practice and refine her hand-eye coordination. Hand-eye coordination is essential for more advanced physical and academic activities. In addition to developing these skills, the pouring activities will also help her understand the concept of conservation of matter. That is, the fact that the same amount of a substance looks different in containers of various sizes and shapes.

To a child this age, remember that work is play, play is work, and learning is not a separate entity. Allow your child to learn through her work of playing at the activities found in this section.

You can help your four-year-old develop her senses by being aware of your sensory perceptions and pointing these out. Be sure to respond favorably when she begins to model this behavior by pointing out to you what she perceives through her senses.

Funnel Pouring with Sand

Materials

- Funnel
- Two large plastic cups
- Sandbox

Activity

This activity should be done in a sandbox. The sandbox will contain the mess and the activity will be more fun. First demonstrate, then help your child do the following. Place the funnel securely in the top of one cup. (Some children prefer small, clear plastic pitchers in the beginning.) Next, scoop up some dry sand in the other cup and slowly pour it into the funnel. After the cup of sand has been poured through the funnel, remove the funnel and place it on the now empty cup. Using the cup containing the sand, pour the sand through the funnel into the other cup. Encourage your child to repeat this activity, pouring back and forth from cup to cup many times.

By using cups or pitchers of different sizes and shapes, your child will begin to grasp the concept that the same amount of a substance looks like a different amount in a different size container.

Funnel Pouring with Colored Water

Materials

- Funnel
- Clear plastic pitchers
- Food coloring
- Water

Activity

Help your child make colored water in one pitcher by filling it half full with water and adding a few drops of food coloring. Watch the water's color change as the food coloring permeates the clear water. Next, help your child place the funnel securely in the top of the empty pitcher. Demonstrate how to slowly pour the colored water through he funnel. Once all the water has been poured through, your child will enjoy repeating the process pouring it back and forth from the containers.

Locks and Keys

Materials

- A few padlocks
- Padlock keys
- Key ring
- Plastic box

Activity

Begin with three padlocks (small, medium, and large) on a key ring. Demonstrate how to try the different keys in each lock until one works, showing how to open each padlock once it is unlocked, and take it off the ring. After all the locks have been opened and removed from the key ring, show your child how to lock them back onto the key ring.

It is not necessary to point out that once a key works for one lock it won't work for the others; let your child discover this for himself. While your child has fun locking and unlocking the locks, he will be developing logical thinking and problem-solving skills.

Bowling

Materials

- Ball
- 6 two-liter plastic bottles

Activity

This fun game teaches a leisure skill while increasing coordination. It can be played inside on a non-carpeted surface or outside when there is no wind.

Show your child how to set up the two-liter bottles as bowling pins, arranging them in a variety of different ways. Count the number of pins (bottles) aloud with your child as you set them up. Then show her how to stand back a few feet and roll the ball (underhand is easiest) toward the pins. Be sure to explain to her that the object of the game is to knock down the pins. You can either have her set up all the pins again after any are knocked down or try to knock down any left standing before resetting them. (The second way is more difficult, so you may want to introduce this option later.) Encourage your child to try this game over and over, and make it more challenging over time by having her move farther and farther back from the pins to roll the ball. A game of skill such as this also presents a good opportunity for you to model for your child the idea of seeing how her skill increases over time, as opposed to comparing her performance to that of others. For example, a comment like, "Wow! Last time you knocked down two pins and now you got four. You're doing great." is a wonderful way to raise her self-esteem.

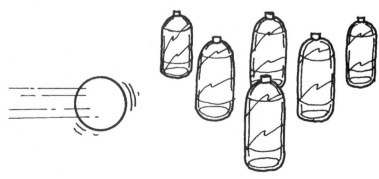

Color Wheel

Materials

- Paper plate
- Paint set
- Paintbrush
- Six clothes pins

Activity

This activity is not only fun to make but becomes another fun learning activity that can be used over and over.

First, mark six small circles or squares of the same size, touching the edge, on a paper plate at the following positions: 2:00, 4:00, 6:00, 8:00, 10:00, and 12:00. Instruct your child to fill in the circles with paint as follows: 2:00 = red, 4:00 = orange, 6:00 = yellow, 8:00 = green, 10:00 = blue, and 12:00 = purple.

Have your child paint both sides of the small, gripping end of each clothespin. Use one color of paint per clothespin, so that you will have one clothespin which corresponds in color to each painted area on the plate.

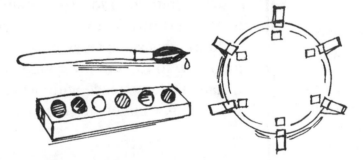

When all the paint is dry, show your child how to clip the clothespins onto the plate so that each clothespin is clipped to the colored area which it matches. Encourage your child to remove all the clothespins and put them all back on again correctly.

In addition to working the hand and finger muscles through opening the clothespins, this activity shows the relationship between primary colors (red, blue, and yellow) and secondary colors (purple, green, and orange), and follows the color pattern of a rainbow.

Making and Using
Play Dough

Materials

- Flour
- Salt
- Water
- Mixing bowl
- Wooden spoon
- Plastic placemat or wax paper
- Cookie cutters
- Aprons or old shirts
- Plastic container
- Rolling pin (Optional)
- Food coloring (Optional)

Activity

Help your child do as much of the mixing as possible, as you mix the ingredients together. Use a wooden spoon at first, then work with your hands, kneading it until the dough is smooth. Talk with your child about the play dough you are making, using and introducing descriptive words such as sticky, smooth, and knead. Once the play dough is made, show him how to roll small pieces into "snakes" using the palm of one hand and a flat surface. Show him how to make balls by rolling a little play dough between both of his palms, and explore making creatures, both human and non-human. Think creatively! Perhaps your child loves dinosaurs and revels the idea of creating his own T-rex. Encourage experimentation!

During this same session, or on another day, show your child how to roll out the dough with a rolling pin and how to flatten a large piece with his hands. Demonstrate how to use cookie cutters to make shapes and pretend cookies.

Recipe for Play Dough

2 cups (480 mL) all-purpose flour
1 cup (240 mL) salt
$^3/_4$ cup (155 mL) water
A few drops of food coloring

This recipe will keep for months if stored in an air-tight container in the refrigerator. It's also made of edible ingredients, so it won't hurt your child if he eats a little.

Tracing Fun

Materials

- Strips of paper
- Dark marker
- Dark, thick crayon

Activity

Draw some various types of lines across the strips of paper. First draw straight lines, then jagged, and finally, curvy. Show your four-year-old how to trace the lines, always moving from the left to the right. Once he masters this, he is ready to try "Scissors Fun."

Scissors Fun

Materials

- Strips of paper
- Dark marker
- Safety scissors

Activity

Using the Tracing Fun activity above, show your child how to cut the lines that you have drawn, starting first with the straight lines and moving on as she masters each. Remember to have her cut from the left to the right, as this is fundamental for early writing and reading skills. Also, the cut strips can be added to your "collage bag," explained and used in the Art Activities section of this book.

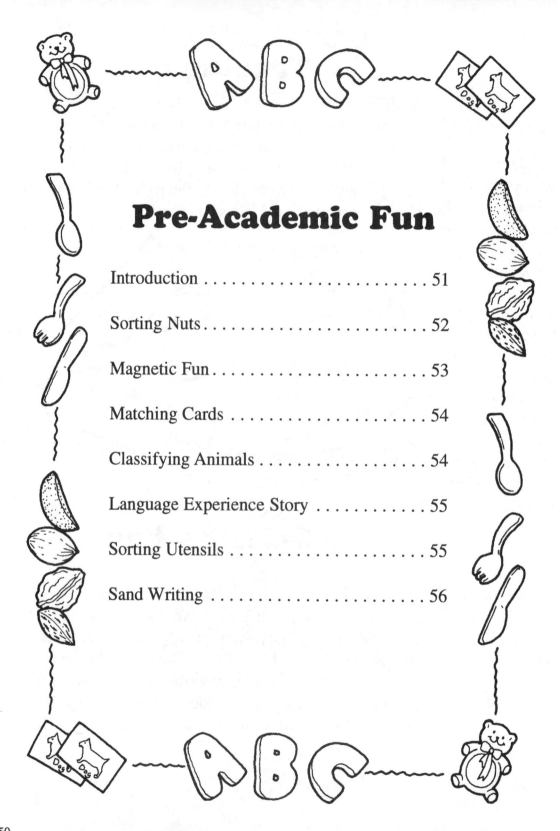

Pre-Academic Fun

Introduction

While all the activities in this book are helpful in terms of your child's development and school-readiness, the activities in this section are directly related to academics, as they teach skills that are prerequisite to academic development and understanding. Helping your child through these activities will help her become a more adept problem-solver and a more observant learner.

It will not be long before your child begins formal schooling, and the time you have together will decrease. The intent of this book is to encourage you to spend time with your four-year-old, having fun while engaging in valuable learning experiences. The more you support her quest for knowledge and discovery, the more she will learn! Though all of the activities in this section are designed to assist your child in becoming ready for school, the best possible thing to do with her is READ! Model reading. Read to her, read with her, listen to taped-recorded stories together, and encourage her to read to you, even though she will most likely just invent the story based on the pictures. These experiences lay the ground work for reading. Create a love for reading. READ!

Sorting Nuts

Materials

- Unshelled nuts
- Container
- Plate with three dividers (Optional)

Activity

Sorting exercises help develop visual discrimination and a sense of logic, both of which are crucial skills for many academic pursuits. After your child is adept at sorting nuts, let her sort other items, such as buttons and beans, too.

Sit with your child and place a bowl of unsorted nuts in front of both of you. (Having four or five of three different types of nuts is a good number to begin with.) Pick up one nut and explain that some of the other nuts look like the one you are holding and some do not. Place the nut in one compartment of the divided plate, or start a pile for this type of nut by placing it to one side of your child. Help and encourage your child to find other nuts that look like the one you have identified and to place them in the same plate compartment or pile. If he finds a different type of nut before finding the same type, point out that it is another type of nut. Help him place it in a different plate compartment or pile. Have him do this for each type, until he has sorted all the nuts into the correct plate compartments or piles.

For more fun, this activity can be expanded after sorting by cracking and tasting one of each type of nut to verify that in addition to looking different, they taste different.

Magnetic Fun

Materials

- Magnet
- Metallic items (i.e., bolts, keys)
- Non-metallic items (i.e., paper, plastic toys)

Activity

This early scientific experiment leads your child to begin drawing conclusions, another important skill in many academic areas.

If your child is not yet familiar with magnets, show her the magnet you will be working with and tell her that it is called a magnet. Explain that some things stick to magnets—and magnets stick to some things—but not everything. Encourage her to experiment with the magnet and the items you have assembled, to see which ones the magnet sticks to or which stick to it, and which ones the magnet will not stick to or will not stick to it. Introduce the idea that some items are "attracted" to the magnet and some are not; likewise, the magnet is "attracted" to some items and not to others. If your child asks why this occurs, explain that only things made out of metal are attracted to or by magnets.

Work with your child to find other household items or toys that are magnetic. This hunt for items that are made of metal will be great fun. However, be sure to use caution and explain that magnets can ruin a television, watch, or computer screen.

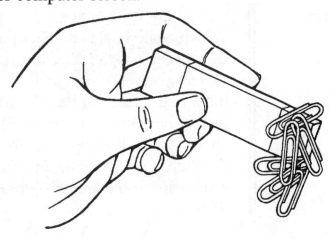

Matching Cards

Materials

- Index cards
- Marker
- Magazine pictures
- Scissors
- Glue

Activity

To assist your child in developing his visual discrimination skills, make six picture cards, two each of three different pictures. (Your child can even help make the cards.) It will help to write the name of the item in the picture on each card, as well. This will allow your child to take a mental picture of the word as he sorts and plays, an early step in the process of learning to read.

Spread out all the cards, with the pictures facing up, in front of your child. Hand him one card and ask him to find another card that looks just the same. When he finds this match, have him set them aside. Repeat this procedure until all cards are matched. When your child has mastered this activity using six cards, gradually increase the number of cards. You can also add more than two cards of each item and have him sort them.

Classifying Animals

Materials

- 10-20 stuffed animals

Activity

Have your child bring all of her stuffed animals out and put them into a big pile. Talk about how they are alike and different. Which are brown? Are any of them soft? Which could be a pet? Grouping by size—big, little, and in-between—is the easiest way to start.

Help your child sort and classify the animals by putting them in the correct pile. For example, "Let's put all of the big ones on the sofa and all of the little ones on the chair." This will help organize your child's logical thinking skills while having fun. Who knows? It might even help get the animals picked up and put away!

Language Experience Story

Materials

- Paper
- Pen
- Crayons
- Stapler

Activity

This is a great activity to follow up a special day, such as a birthday party, trip to the zoo, or lunch at Grandma's. Tell your child that the two of you are going to write a story about the special day you had. Try to get your child to do most of the story telling as you write down what she says. Divide the story up on the paper as you write it, so that there are just a couple of sentences to each page. When your child has finished telling you what to write, read each page back to her one at a time.

Encourage your child to illustrate each page and praise her story writing abilities with comments like, "Wow! You have told the story so nicely it's going to be a beautiful book! I'm sure everyone will want to read it and see your pretty pictures." After your child illustrates the pages and you staple the story together, you will have a brand new story to read, written by your child's favorite author—herself.

Sorting Utensils

Materials

- Spoons
- Forks
- Dull dinner knives
- Silverware organizer

Activity

This fun, useful activity can help grown-ups get work done and little ones feel big. When unloading the dishwasher, simply ask your four-year-old to take charge of the silverware holder. (Be sure to remove anything sharp before giving it to your child.) Using the silverware sorter, your child can sit at the table and put the utensils in the correct area. Not only will the silverware get put away, your child will get valuable practice with sorting, a math skill.

Sand Writing

Materials

- Two plastic trays
- Sand

Activity

Writing in sand, which is easier than writing on paper, begins to train the hand and the eyes for writing on paper. It is also a fun way to practice writing the alphabet letters and drawing pictures. Simply give your child a tray filled halfway with sand and demonstrate how to "write" in the sand with your index finger. Start by drawing a circle, then encourage your child to do the same using her sand tray. (Don't worry if your child switches hands during early writing activities such as this. It is normal.) Gradually move on to making more complex shapes, then to making capital letters for your child to copy. Always allow your child to look at your example when making her shapes or letters. If it helps, you can even make yours one step at a time and let your child copy as you go.

Sand Writing Progression

- ✔ + (plus mark)
- ✔ △ triangle
- ✔ ☐ square
- ✔ curved letters (C, G, J)
- ✔ straight line letters (T, I, L, X)
- ✔ other capital letters

Be sure to let your child lead and make marks and shapes for you to copy, too. For variety, try using dry coffee grounds, salt, rice, or flour, in place of sand. Also, you may wish to use a large sand tray for this activity so that your child can practice making more than one letter or symbol at a time.

Nature Activities

Introduction

Most children are fascinated by nature, so the activities in this section serve to enhance your child's understanding of the world of nature by expanding his scientific knowledge. While broadening his understanding of how natural occurrences like flower and butterfly growth take place, these activities will show your child how nature's calendar is constantly changing. They will help him begin to understand that the world is an evolving, ever-changing place. This understanding can lead your child to respect and appreciate nature, resulting in a lifetime of peaceful coexistence as he interacts with plants, animals, and other natural phenomena.

You can use the planting activities in this section as a starting point. If your child enjoys planting things, why not help him plant an entire small garden of flowers, fruits, or vegetables? If your child enjoys "Classifying Leaves," why not classify other items found in nature? And if he likes "Cocoon Watching," try to help him find a bird nest to watch from a safe distance with binoculars.

Magnifying Glass

Materials

- Plastic magnifying glass
- Insects
- Leaves

Activity

Go outside and help your child hold the magnifying glass over a moving insect. Slowly move the glass as the insect moves. If the insect goes away, magnify leaves instead. Introduce or reinforce the concepts of "big/bigger" and "small/smaller" as you help your child observe. Encourage her to talk about other things she notices. Also, introduce the vocabulary words "insect" and "magnifying glass," as children this age take pride in learning the real words for things.

Classifying Leaves

Materials

- Leaves
- Paper (Optional)
- Paste or glue (Optional)

Activity

This activity is beneficial because classifying develops the logical mind and helps prepare children to read and to understand math by noting similarities and differences.

Go outdoors and collect some leaves—between 10 and 20 will be great. If weather permits, find a level surface and do your classifying outside; otherwise, go inside to find a work space. Encourage your child to talk about some of the individual leaves that you collected together. If your child is hesitant, ask questions such as "What color is this one?" or "Do you have a leaf that is very big?" After a while, ask other questions like "Can you find any more leaves the color of this one?" Lead your child to put the leaves in groups according to certain characteristics such as color or size.

You may want to extend this activity by pasting or gluing some of the groupings on paper.

Planting Seeds

Materials

- Corn seeds
- Empty aquarium or clear container
- Potting soil

Activity

The method of planting seeds provides your child with a unique opportunity to see what happens both above and below the earth's surface as plants grow.

Help your child fill an aquarium (or other container such as a plastic, two-liter soda bottle) with about four inches (10 cm.) of potting soil. Help her make ¹/₂ inch (2.54 cm.) deep indentations in the soil with one finger, next to the edge, approximately every three inches (7.62 cm.), along one side of the aquarium. Next, help her put a few seeds into each indentation. Then help her pack about ¹/₂ inch (2.54 cm.) of soil on top of the seeds. Help her sprinkle the entire aquarium with enough water so that the top is moist. Set the aquarium in a sunny window (seeded side to the light) and help her water it twice daily. Encourage her each day to look closely at the side where she planted the seeds, helping her notice growth both above and below the soil. Guide her to understand that the soil line in the aquarium is like the Earth's surface outside and that, in this case, we can see (through the glass or plastic) things occurring below the surface which we cannot see in the ground outside.

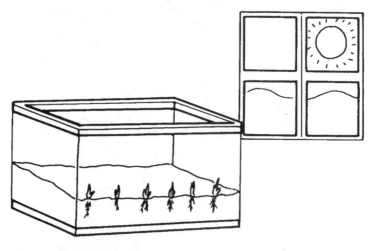

Planting Flowers

Materials

- Small flowers
- Small trowel
- Area for planting

Activity

Children can grow intellectually and spiritually through nurturing living, growing things. Get three to five small flowers like marigolds or zinnias and let your child have the wonderful opportunity of planting and caring for flowers.

Help your child dig a hole just slightly larger than the plug of soil surrounding the plant. Set the plant inside the hole, and cover around the plant with the soil removed from the hole. When all the plants are in the ground, help your child to gently water them. Watering should be done daily to keep the soil moist. (This makes a wonderful job for a four-year-old!) When the flowers are large enough, let your child decide when and if she wants to pick them.

Cocoon Watching

Materials

- Jar with lid
- Caterpillar or stick with cocoon attached

Activity

Watching a butterfly emerge from a cocoon is an incredible experience for a four-year-old! The hard part for you will be to find a cocoon to let your child observe. The best advice is to find a caterpillar, give him a lot of food, and watch him build a cocoon.

Secure the caterpillar or stick with a cocoon attached inside a jar. Be sure to poke holes in the lid of the jar first. (A cricket keeper will also work in lieu of a jar.) Emphasize to your child that this cocoon stage is like a sleeping stage, so the jar or cricket keeper needs to be kept very still. Explain to him that four things must happen to make a butterfly.

1. A butterfly lays eggs, out of which come
2. caterpillars which have to eat a lot, then spin themselves into
3. cocoons where they will sleep while they get ready to emerge as
4. butterflies.

Be sure to discuss before and during this activity the facts. In the caterpillar stage, this animal needs a lot of space in which to crawl around and eat leaves. Also, once the butterfly comes out of the cocoon, it will need to be released within a couple of hours so that it has room to fly.

Encourage your child to look at the jar a few times a day to see if anything has happened. To ease the waiting, your child might like to illustrate the four stages in the life cycle of the butterfly. A great book to supplement this activity (especially during the waiting period) is *The Very Hungry Caterpillar,* by Eric Carle, listed in the resource section of this book.

Away From Home

Introduction

Being away from home can certainly present challenges for four-year-olds and their parents. The key to keeping everyone happy is to plan ahead and employ activities such as those listed in this section. The activities here are especially good for traveling and restaurant visits, both trying times for most four-year-olds. As mentioned in the introduction to this book, your four-year-old needs help in understanding which behaviors are appropriate in which situations. The activities in this section will help her learn appropriate, constructive ways to spend her time and energy in some different settings. Use these fun activities to help ensure that time spent away from home is a happy time for everyone.

The While Traveling part of this section includes the song "The Wheels on the Car." This song is only one of many that can be sung while traveling. Singing songs again and again over time develops your child's memory and sense of logic and sequencing. "Mystery Bag" is a quieter activity that will provide your child with more fun, yet is purposeful and will engage your child while traveling.

The Restaurant Activities part of this section can mean the difference between a stressful family dinner and a "good time had by all." The combination of independent activities such as "Coloring My Food" and group activities like "I Spy" can help your four-year-old feel a part of the group as well as help her learn to entertain herself.

The Wheels on the Car

Activity

Materials

- Words to song (See below.)

Singing songs again and again, over time develops your child's memory and sense of logical sequence. After your child learns all the verses, encourage her to make up more verses with your help. This will give her a sense of accomplishment and show her that she can create valid things. . . not all knowledge must come from grown-ups.

This song has some optional hand motions which you may want to teach your child before the car ride. Remember, many other songs are also suitable for singing in the car. For example, singing "A-E-I-O-U" or reciting some of the body poems in the Music and Movement section are excellent ways to constructively occupy your four-year-old while traveling in the car.

Words and actions to "The Wheels on the Car"

(sung to the tune of "The Wheels on the Bus")

Verse 1: The wheels on the car go round and round, round and round, round and round;
The wheels on the car go round and round, all through the town.
Action: Roll bent forearms over each other, held in front of your body.

Verse 2: The wipers on the car go swish-swish-swish, swish-swish-swish, swish-swish-swish;
The wipers on the car go swish-swish-swish, all through the town.
Action: Hold both palms in front of you and twist your wrists back and forth.

Verse 3: The windows on the car go up and down, up and down, up and down;
The windows on the car go up and down, all through the town.
Action: Move arms up and down, bending at the elbow.

Verse 4: The horn on the car goes beep-beep-beep, beep-beep-beep, beep-beep-beep;
The horn on the car goes beep-beep-beep, all through the town.
Action: Push one fist out in front of you and move it as if knocking on a door.

Mystery Bag

Materials

- Drawstring cloth bag
- Small items (i.e., toothbrush, toys, sock, cotton ball, key, sea shell)

Activity

This activity develops your child's kinesthetic awareness and refines his sense of touch. Although it is listed under travel activities, this is also a good restaurant activity.

Before setting out on your trip, show your child the items which are going in the mystery bag. Allow him to help select items and begin with just four or five. Be sure he knows the name of each item and have him feel each one before it goes into the bag. While on your trip, name an item from the bag and have your child reach inside without looking and feel around to find it. Your child should pull out the object so you can both see it. This object should be put back in the bag to keep the game challenging while your child searches for the next object you name. (Some very independent children may choose to play this game alone by feeling inside the bag for an object, guessing what it is, and pulling it out to be sure; it is fine if your child chooses to play this way. Enjoy the time on your own.)

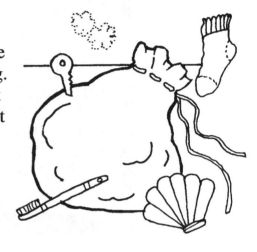

Once your child is comfortable with this activity in its original form, gradually add more items to the bag or change all of the items in the bag. You can also try not showing your child the items beforehand to increase the challenge even more.

Coloring My Food

Materials

- Paper plate
- Crayons

Activity

This activity is more exciting and educational than just coloring the placemat. It often turns eating out into an enjoyable experience with a four-year-old!

Once your child's meal has been ordered, you can begin. Discuss with her what she ordered and what it will look like on her plate. Help her think about colors by asking questions like, " What color will your applesauce be?" Then help her as needed, while she draws and colors on the paper plate what her meal will look like.

If you are going to a restaurant notorious for long waits or a new one where you're not sure how long the wait will be, arm yourself with a few extra plates and encourage your child to draw or color the meals that other family members have ordered, too.

I Spy

Materials

- None

Activity

Here is a new twist on an old game. This version helps increase your child's vocabulary and knowledge of food and food-related objects.

First define your boundaries, such as "We will be playing this game with things on our table only." Then tell your child that this is a special kind of guessing game and that the words "I spy" mean the same thing as "I see." Give your child a couple of examples before beginning. Tell her that, if, for instance, you said, "I spy a yellow vegetable" she could guess that it was the corn on Daddy's plate. Point out that someone could spy napkins, cups, silverware, etc.

Naming Foods and Their Colors

Materials

• The family's dinner plates

Activity

There are two different ways to do this activity. Using the first way, talk about each person's dinner separately, going around the table. For example, "Your brother Johnny has peas for his vegetable. Do you know what color his peas are?" Give your four-year-old time to respond, then reinforce by saying, "Yes, the peas are green." If your four-year-old cannot name the color, you or Johnny can tell what color the peas are. Then say, "And for his main dish, Johnny has spaghetti with sauce on it." Let Johnny point to his spaghetti. Then ask your four-year-old, "Can you tell us what color Johnny's spaghetti sauce is?" Reinforce the correct answer as above, repeating the correct color word. After you have finished talking about Johnny's dinner, move on to another person's dinner, and so on, around the table.

The second way to use this activity is to talk about each food group separately, going plate by plate, around the table. If you choose to use this second method, name the food group you are discussing as you move from plate to plate. For example, "Your brother Johnny has peas for his vegetable." Have Johnny point to his peas and ask your four-year-old what color Johnny's peas are. Then move around the table talking about the next person's vegetable(s), being sure to use the word "vegetable" each time. Continue in this manner with everyone's vegetables, then move on to another food group.

In either method used, it is not necessary to talk about everything on everyone's plate, but do be sure that you do talk about all the food on your four-year-old's plate.

Letter and Number I.D.

Materials

- Restaurant menu

Activity

On the menu, point to a certain letter or number with which your child is familiar. Review the name of this letter or number with your child. Then ask him to search the rest of the menu and show you where he sees that same letter or number again. Reinforce his correct answers by saying, "Yes, that is a _____," (for example "two"). Challenge him to find more than one of the letters or numbers he is looking for, then once each letter or number has been exhausted, or your child is ready for a change, point out another letter or number for him to find on the menu.

This activity can be expanded into an ABC Race, similar to the popular license plate game played in the car, where your child can attempt to find all of the letters of the alphabet, or all numbers from 1–10.

The World of Make-Believe

Introduction

Just as you do, your four-year-old learns through keeping an open mind. Exercises in make-believe help keep the mind open and the imagination in practice. This helps develop the ability to solve problems and think abstractly; these abilities will help your child learn today and everyday for the rest of her life. So, as you play with your child through the activities in this section, understand that you are doing much more than just playing; you are preparing your child for the future.

There is much to be learned through practicing different roles, a skill used in "Dress-Up" and "Camping Out." Other activities in this section, like "Puppet Show," allow your child to visit another place without ever leaving the comfort and security of home.

As you embark on a make-believe journey with your child, relish the development of her imagination. Whether you are Jasmine and Aladdin flying on a magic carpet or ballerinas dancing in a show, play with your child and encourage her to create wonderful experiences for the two of you to enjoy!

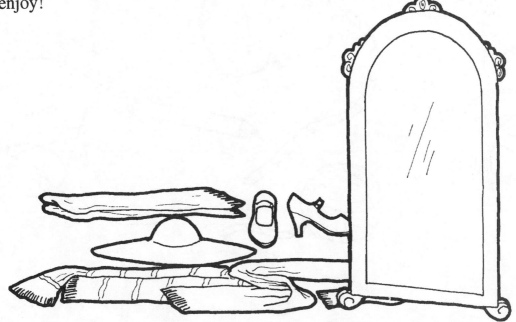

String Telephone

Materials

- Two styrofoam cups
- Pencil
- String

Activity

Help your child punch a hole in the bottom of each cup with a pencil. Help him put about two yards (1.82 m) of string through each end. Tie a knot in the string at each end of the phone so that it won't slip out of the holes. Show your child how to play telephone with the cups. Put one cup to his mouth to talk and one to his ear to listen. Take turns modeling and talking to yourselves and then dive into a full blown conversation by having one of you talk into one phone while the other listens on the other end. This "give and take" sharing can help him learn ways to share and wait his turn while the two of you enjoy your own phone conversation.

Puppet Show

Materials

- Hand puppets (Homemade or commercial)
- Puppet stage (Optional)

Activity

Puppet play allows your child to try out being different characters, as does playing dress-up, but puppet play also lends itself to storytelling.

Demonstrate for your child how to put the puppets on your hands and how to use different voices for each puppet. Remember, homemade puppets are just as fun and can be made with socks, paper sacks, or paper and craft sticks. In fact, this activity can begin with a puppet making time. You can also build a puppet stage by standing a large box on its end and cutting off the back, making a three-sided frame. Then, cut out a rectangle in the front to create a "stage" area through which the puppets can be seen. Or, tape a blanket across a doorway at your child's waist level and use it as the stage. Regardless, encourage him to retell a story he knows or to create a whole new story as he works with the puppets.

If you have the opportunity to take your child to watch a real puppet show, it can serve to reinforce his concept of puppet play, as well as be an exciting experience.

Camping Out

Materials

- Room with furniture
- Blanket or sheet

Activity

If your child likes to camp, suggest a make-believe trip right now to practice. Help her create a "tent" by throwing an old sheet or blanket over some furniture so that it hangs down and you can crawl in and out. Pretend to assemble firewood, make a fire, put marshmallows on sticks, and roast them in the fire. Continue pretending, being sure to fish and hike. Also, take advantage of the chance to talk about safety in your pretend camping trip to help set the tone for a real camping trip one day.

Dress-Up

Materials

- Clothes
- Scarves
- Ties
- Shoes
- Hats
- Large mirror (Optional)

Activity

As their identities are emerging, four-year-olds love to act like other people. Dressing up and then looking in the mirror provides the perfect opportunity for your child to play at being someone else.

Provide your child with many old clothes. (Items like shirts, dresses, pants, and skirts that are no longer being used by an older child or adult are perfect.) Encourage her to try on different outfits. Remember this is the world of make-believe, so anything goes. For example, cowboy boots with a baseball cap and sequined dress are fine together. In addition to just trying on different outfits, allow and encourage your child to act like the character which she is dressed up as. Ask questions such as, "Who (or what) are you being now?" Encourage your child to look in the mirror to see how she looks in these different costumes.

Bear Hunt

Materials

• Teddy bears

Activity

Using three or four teddy bears to begin, simply take turns hiding and finding the bears. This can be done outside, but is a good activity to save for a rainy day when you are stuck in the house because it can provide lots of indoor fun.
This also works well when older children play the game with your four-year-old as they can model good places to hide and strategies for finding the bears. Increase the number of bears you hunt for as your child gets better or gains interest in the game.

My Zoo

Materials

• Stuffed animals

Activity

Help your child create her own zoo by placing her stuffed animals in different spots around the yard or house. Help her incorporate things like plants or trees in making appropriate habitats for her animals. For example, a toy giraffe would like to be eating from a tree, a turtle would prefer to be in grass or low green plants, and a monkey would like toys and trees. This activity can be as elaborate as your child wants. Encourage her to use her imagination in providing dishes of food and water for her animals. Perhaps you and other family members can come visit your child's zoo.

Bibliography of Resources

Ames, Bates. *Your Four-Year-Old.* Delta Books, 1976.

Baldwin, Rahima. *You Are Your Child's First Teacher.* Celestial Arts, 1989.

Bavolek, Juliana. *Nurturing Book for Babies and Children.* Family Development Resources, Inc., 1989.

Cantor, Pamela. *Understanding a Child's World.* McGraw Hill Book Co., 1977.

Dinkmeyer, Dinkmeyer, & McKay. *Parenting Young Children.* American Guidance Service, 1989.

Ellison, Sheila, & Judith Gray. *365 Days of Creative Play.* Sourcebooks, Inc., 1995.

MacGregor, Cynthia. *Raising a Creative Child.* Carol Publishing Group, 1996.

Montessori, Maria. *The Absorbent Mind.* Dell Publishing Co., Inc., 1984.

Salk, Lee. *What Every Child Would Like His Parents to Know.* David McKay Co., 1972.

Singer & Revson. *A Piaget Primer: How a Child Thinks.* Penguin Books, U.S.A., Inc., 1978.

Bibliography of Children's Books

Bernthal, M. *Baby Bop Goes to School.* The Lyons Group, 1994.

Bridwell, N. *Clifford the Big Red Dog.* Scholastic, 1974. This is the first of many Clifford books that will entertain your child. Look for other Clifford books at your local library.

Carle, E. All of Eric Carle's books are excellent for four-year-olds. Try *The Very Busy Spider; The Very Hungry Caterpillar; Brown Bear, Brown Bear, What Do You See?; Polar Bear, Polar Bear, What Do You Hear?;* and *123 at the Zoo.*

Carlstrom, N.W. *Wild Wild Sunflower Child Anna.* Macmillan Publishing Company, 1987.

Dowdy, L.C. *Barney Goes to the Zoo.* The Lyons Group, 1993.

Dowdy, L.C. *Happy Birthday Baby Bop!* The Lyons Group, 1993.

Josse, B.M. *Mama, Do You Love Me?* Penguin, 1993.

Krauss, R. *The Carrot Seed.* Harper & Row Publishers, Inc., 1945.

Martin, B. & J. Archambault *Chicka Chicka Boom Boom.* Simon & Schuster, 1989.

Numeroff, L.J. *If You Give a Mouse a Cookie.* HarperCollins Publishers, 1990.

Numeroff, L.J. *If You Give a Moose a Muffin.* HarperCollins Publishers, 1991.

Pfister, M. *The Rainbow Fish.* North-South Books, Inc., 1996.

Rey, H. A. *Curious George.* Houghton Mifflin Co., 1952. (The entire Curious George series is a delightful set for four-year-olds.)

Seuss, Dr. All Dr. Seuss books are great for introducing rhyming words while having fun!

Wood, A. *The Napping House.* Harcourt Brace Jovanovich Publishers, 1984.

Bibliography of Music

Basic Rhythms #1, cassette tape can be ordered from Kay Ortmans Productions, 11667 Alba Rd., Ben Lomand, CA 95005.

Buckwheat Zydeco. "Choo Choo Boogaloo." *Music for Little People Sampler: A Joyful Collection of Songs from Around the World.* Lawndale, CA: Music for Little People, 1994.

Cassidy, N. *"Kid's Songs."* Klutz, 1986.

Cockburn, V., & Steinbergh, J. "Where I Come From!" *Songs and Poems from Many Cultures.* Chestnut Hill, MA: Talking Stone Press, 1991.

"Let's Sing Happy Songs." Metacom, Inc., 1991.

McCutcheon, J. "Skip to my Lou." *A Child's Celebration of Song.* Lawndale, CA: Music for Little People.

McGrath, B., & K. Smithrium, *Songs and Games for Toddlers.* Toronto, Ontario: Kids' Records,1985.

Raffi. "Riding in an Airplane" and "One Light, One Sun." Hollywood, CA: A & M Records.

Rocking Round the Zoo. Cassette tape can be ordered from GT Audio Corp. 16 East 40th Street, New York, NY 10016.

Wee Sing Silly Songs. Price Stern Sloan, 1982. (This entire series of tapes is a delightful set for four-year-olds.)

Other Resources

Center for Music and Young Children, 217 Nassau Street, Princeton, NJ 08542. Write for a free brochure and catalog.

Disney—most Disney movies have wonderful soundtracks available. *Rhythm of the Pride Lands* from *The Lion King* and *Sebastian the Crab* from *The Little Mermaid* are excellent examples of selections that your four-year-old is sure to love!

Peg Hoenack's Music Works, 8409 Seven Locks Road, Bethesda, MD 20817-2006. (They provide materials that combine music training with other skills.)

"Young Person's Guide to the Orchestra," Benjamin Britten.